D1403906

Nancy Ward, Cherokee

OTHER BOOKS BY HAROLD W. FELTON

Legends of Paul Bunyan
Pecos Bill: Texas Cowpuncher
John Henry and His Hammer
Fire-Fightin' Mose
Bowleg Bill: Seagoing Cowpuncher
Cowboy Jamboree: Western Songs and Lore
New Tall Tales of Pecos Bill
Mike Fink: Best of the Keelboatmen
A Horse Named Justin Morgan
Sergeant O'Keefe and His Mule, Balaam
William Phips and the Treasure Ship
Pecos Bill and the Mustang
Jim Beckwourth, Negro Mountain Man
Edward Rose, Negro Trail Blazer
True Tall Tales of Stormalong
Nat Love, Negro Cowboy
Big Mose: Hero Fireman
Mumbet: The Story of Elizabeth Freeman
James Weldon Johnson
Gib Morgan, Oil Driller
Ely S. Parker: Spokesman for the Senecas

Nancy Ward, Cherokee

HAROLD W. FELTON

Illustrated by Carolyn Bertrand

DODD, MEAD & COMPANY
New York

Map on pages 16-17 by Salem Tamer

Library of Congress Cataloging in Publication Data

Felton, Harold W   1902-
   Nancy Ward, Cherokee.

   Includes index.
   1. Ward, Nancy, d. 1822—Juvenile literature.
I. Bertrand, Carolyn, ill.
E99.C5W263   973.3'092'4 [B]   74-25512
ISBN 0-396-07072-8

To Myrtle Williamson

CONTENTS

PREFACE

THE RECOGNITION that Nancy Ward once had is almost gone, a strange fate for a woman who played a heroic part in the success of the American Revolution.

Nancy Ward was a Ghigau or "Beloved Woman" of the Cherokees. It was a title earned by her conduct in her nation's interest. Her people gave her a leading place in their councils.

In her time the Cherokees wrote no history. It was carried in memory and tradition. But the white men, traders, soldiers, and government agents, in their letters and reports, left a tantalizingly incomplete, yet reasonably satisfying record of her.

James Robertson, North Carolina's agent to the Overhill Cherokees, described her as "queenly and commanding," and reported that her house was furnished in accordance with her high dignity, in barbaric splendor.

James Mooney, in *Myths of the Cherokee*, characterizes her as "noted." A. V. Goodpasture, in *Indian War and Warriors*, calls her "famous" and writes that she "was a consistent advocate of peace, and constant in her good offices to both races."

Thomas Nuttall, the famous botanist, visited the Arkansas Cherokees in 1819 and gives a physical description of her as "tall, erect, and beautiful, with a prominent nose, regular features, clear complexion, long, silken black hair, large, piercing black eyes, and an imperious air."

Nancy Ward would have been well over eighty years old at the time Nuttall wrote, and, as he clearly describes a much younger woman, it must be concluded that he gained his information from oral sources. Heroines can stay young in tradition. He observes that she was called "Beloved" by way of eminence and esteem, and he comments that "from her have sprung men of distinction, by whose influence and example the condition of their Indian brethren has been ameliorated."

General Joseph Martin married one of her daughters. William, his white son by a former marriage, called Nancy Ward "one of the most superior women I have ever met." Other contemporary accounts use similar descriptions. She has been called the "Cherokee Pocahontas." Thomas Jefferson, as governor of Virginia, took notice of her assistance to the American cause in the Revolutionary War.

There is a common notion that the Cherokees were opposed to the embattled colonials. That is an easy generality caused by oversimplification. There was a substantial peace party among the Cherokees and Nancy Ward was one of its leaders. R. S.

Cotterill, in *The Southern Indians*, writes, "The great majority of the Cherokees remained at peace." The *Encyclopaedia Britannica* also recognizes this division of opinion.

In a time when some members of an Indian nation were conducting a fiercely aggressive war, a peace party is easily overlooked by its harried opponents. Yet Nancy Ward was right there, yearning for peace, but supporting the Americans every inch of the way.

Nancy Ward's World

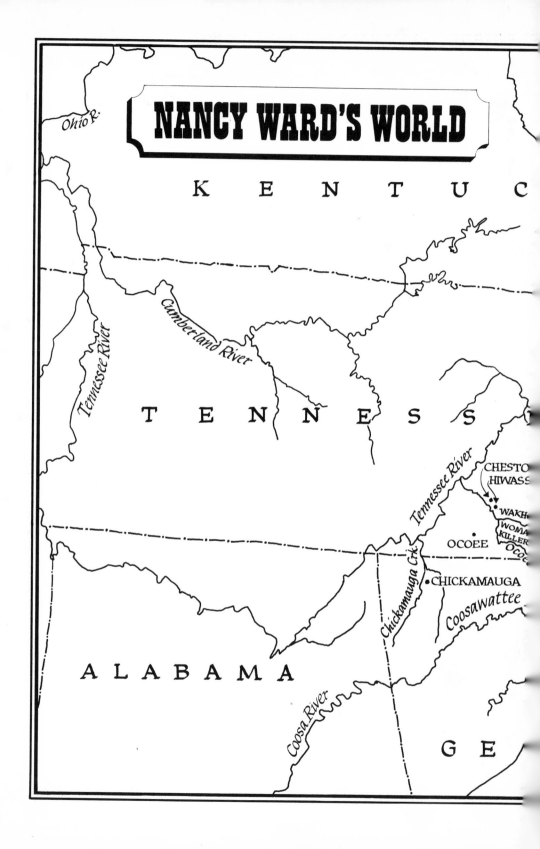

WEST
VIRGINIA

VIRGINIA

K Y

Cumberland Mts.

Cumberland
Gap

Powell River

Clinch-River

Carter's Valley

Long Island of Holston

New River

• FT. CHISWELL

• FT. WATAUGA

Sycamore Shoals

Watauga River

Holston River

Notichucky River

NORTH
CAROLINA

E

LLICO BLOCKHOUSE

OTA

CHILHOWEE

SETTICO

LICO

Little Tenn. R.

Great Smoky Mts.

French Broad River

Boyd's Creek

HUNGRY
CAMP

ssee R.

HOPEWELL

Keowee River

Saluda River

SOUTH
CAROLINA

ahoochee River

Tugaloo River

Savannah River

G I A

Tamer

Nancy Ward, Cherokee

Chapter I

NANYE'HI

ON A DAY in the 1730s a baby girl was born. Who can know what day? No record of her birth can now be found. But she left a record of her life in the memories of her people and on the pages of history.

Her mother was Tame Doe, of the Wolf Clan of the Cherokees, and a sister of Chief Attakullaculla. Her father was Sir Francis Ward, an English soldier.

Her Indian name was Nanye'hi. Her English name was Nancy. Nancy Ward. As a baby, she was called Wild Rose, because her skin was dark and pink and soft, like the wild flower that grew in the land of the Cherokees.

In those old days the Cherokees hunted in the land south of the Ohio River, south to a place beyond the Tennessee River, deep into the headwaters of the Coosa, the Chattahoochee, the Savannah, the Saluda, and the Tugaloo rivers.

It was a rich and beautiful land of mountains, hills, forests,

streams, and valleys. Its heart was at the edge of the Great
Smoky Mountains which rest as a crown at the heights in the
region where the states of Tennessee, Georgia, South Carolina,
and North Carolina now come together and where sweet, fresh
streams give birth to the rivers that flow to the west and to the
south and east.

It was here that Nancy Ward was born, at a town called
Chota, the capital of the Cherokees, on the Little Tennessee
River. It was a "City of Refuge," where the hunted and those in
distress knew they would be protected.

It was an area the coming years were to fill with tumult and
war.

Her father died and Nancy did not remember him. Tame
Doe taught her English and Cherokee, two languages, a great
gift for any child. And Tame Doe taught her the ways of two
worlds that were coming closer and closer together, the world
of the white men and the world of the Indians.

Chapter 2

THE WHITE ROAD

A TIME came when childhood games began to seem dull. It was a time when friendship between a boy and a girl changed.

The girl was Nanye'hi. The boy was Kingfisher, of the Deer Clan. She was slender and beautiful. He was straight and tall and strong.

He could fish and hunt. He was young, but he was a brave, a warrior, a man. He could care for and protect a home and family. He could bring home meat and skins and furs.

She was young too, but she was a woman. She had strength and courage. She could make a home. She could raise a garden, prepare meals, tan hides, make clothing, rear a family.

Her smiling black eyes and his flashing black eyes that had met so often in friendship and play now met in another fashion, in close affection.

They found ways to be together, alone. Other friends became less important to them.

And then Kingfisher said, "My footprints have come to meet the white pathways that lie before you."

Nanye'hi knew the turn of his mind and she was glad. It was a Cherokee declaration, full of meaning. In their tradition, white was good. White pathways meant a happy future together for a man and woman. It had been so ever since the Great Spirit had sent them to their sacred land.

But she knew that on their white pathways, in their happy future, there would be some sadness. "Sorrow and lonely pathways lie before us too," she said.

"At my back upon the eternal white road will be the sound of your footsteps. I have just come to draw away your soul," he said.

"Then your thoughts are not to wander away. Your soul is to be mine," she said.

There was no red in him. Red signified war, just as white meant peace and happiness to the Cherokees. He was not a coward. He would fight to protect himself and his family, as a man must—and she would too. But they would search out and they would cling to the white road.

The words they had said were old words. The two young people had heard them in stories and in rituals. Now it was their time to repeat the ancient phrases, for love had come to them.

Chapter 3

THE MARRIAGE

On the day set for the marriage, they appeared before the people of the village. There were over a hundred Cherokee towns, and people came from them too. The Wolf and the Deer Clans would be drawn closer.

It was a happy day. Nanye'hi and Kingfisher were both dressed in white deerskin, decorated with colored beads and tassels and porcupine quills.

Her shining black hair was drawn to the top of her head and fastened with a silver pin. His head was shaved, except for a crown lock at the top and back. It was decorated with beads and a few long eagle feathers.

Kingfisher gave Nanye'hi a haunch of venison, a sign of his power and his desire to hunt for her. She gave him an ear of corn, a symbol of her eagerness to be a good housekeeper for him.

There were a few words. "I have just come to you, King-fisher," she said softly.

"No loneliness," he said.

"Think of me without loneliness," she said.

"Think of me from your very soul," he replied.

"The white road is open before us," she declared.

"The white road is the way that leads to a happy future."

Then the feasting came and the laughing and the dancing. Old friendships were sharpened with those who came from the other towns, widely separated, in the vast Cherokee lands.

It was over. They were man and wife.

Chapter 4

THE BELOVED WOMAN

THE YEARS passed—enough years to bring two children. A boy named Five Killer and a girl, Catharine.

There had been times of peace, when hunters went out and came back with meat for the fire, with hides and furs for clothing and blankets. There had been years when the fields were filled with corn and beans and squash, when the cooking fires burned brightly and bellies were full.

There had been the red times also, times of war—for war was never far away from the Cherokees. The braves went out on the warpath after drinking the "black drink" for success. Some of the men returned with victory or defeat, glory or shame. Some did not return.

Among the Cherokees, women voted in the councils that met to consider war. Who had a better right to take part in such a question? It was their sons, husbands, and fathers who faced the dangers of war.

And among the Cherokees, women often went to war with the men. Sadly, but proudly, Nanye'hi followed the footsteps of her husband, Kingfisher, when the Creeks attacked from the south. She went with him to receive the enemy.

The battle raged. The Creeks came. They were driven back. They came again. Nanye'hi, at Kingfisher's side, helped him. She made ready the powder, the packing, and the balls. She chewed on the lead balls to make them strong, to make them win.

In the midst of battle, an evil bullet, bearing death, flew between the small white birch trees, sped over the green grass, beneath the blue sky, and found the red blood in Kingfisher's heart. He fell.

Nanye'hi took up his weapon and used it against the enemy. The Cherokee warriors saw her, and stronger hearts came to them, and a new spirit.

Nanye'hi rose and advanced. The warriors came too. The Creeks fled.

Upon their return to the Cherokee capital, the stories of the battle were told and there was a dance of victory.

Then an ancient Cherokee ceremony was performed, and Nanye'hi was made Ghigau, a "Beloved Woman" of the nation. It was a place of greatest honor, occupied only by women who had distinguished themselves. Forever after she would sit in the highest councils of the Cherokee nation. In every great decision her voice would be heard.

Chapter 5

THE CLOUDS OF WAR

THE DARK clouds of the American Revolutionary War were gathering. Strife was building between the white men, between those who ruled in England and those who were ruled in America.

English agents sought the land of the Cherokees as did the white Americans who were beginning to dream of their freedom. The Cherokees held to their own dreams of liberty.

Large tracts of land had been taken in trade for knives and axes, pots and pans, beads and dyes, blankets of wool and cotton cloth, and guns and lead and powder—and, unfortunately, for whisky. The Cherokees needed or wanted such items of trade. They gave their land for manufactured goods, and often whisky was the cause and the reason for the trade.

The treaties were signed with the marks of some of the chiefs or important men. Often those men were first made drunk, or bribed. But no person owned the Cherokee land, no chief, no important man. It was owned by all of the Cherokees.

Small tracts of land were taken by settlers—just simply taken—no trade at all.

Some traders were good and honest men, delivering trade goods in fair amount for skins and furs and produce. Some were evil men, ready to cheat their red brothers.

Alexander Cameron, an agent of the English King, said in 1768, "No nation was ever infested with such a set of villains and horse thieves. A trader will invent and tell a thousand lies; and stir up trouble against all other white persons that he judges rivals in trade."

In the same year, the Cherokee chief, Oconostota, said bitterly, after one hundred square miles of land had been traded to the English, "We have now given the white men enough land to live on."

In the passing of the years, Nanye'hi's first love for Kingfisher drowned itself in sorrow. Her white pathway had been cut by death and war. But another opened. Another love was born. This was for Bryant Ward, a nephew of her father. There was another marriage ceremony.

In time, a daughter Elizabeth was born, and a son, Little Fellow.

Chapter 6

A VOICE FOR PEACE

IN MARCH, 1775, the Cherokees met with agents of the Transylvania Company at Sycamore Shoals, high in the headwaters of the Tennessee River, on the Watauga. The Battle of Bunker Hill and Paul Revere's midnight ride occurred that same spring.

Two questions arose in the Cherokee councils. Should more land be sold to the English Transylvania Company? What part should the Cherokees play in the rapidly developing strife between the American colonials and the English King?

These questions divided Cherokee families and clans in the same fashion that loyalty to the King was dividing the white people.

Because they lacked enough guns and ammunition, the Cherokees had suffered a defeat at the hands of the Chickasaws in the south. The arrows of former times were no answer to an enemy supplied with guns by the English.

34

White settlers were constantly coming, and slowly they were settling in the treasured Cherokee lands on the Watauga, Holston, and Nolichucky rivers—in spite of a treaty with the English and a Royal Proclamation of 1763, which reserved the country west of the Appalachian Mountains as hunting grounds for the Indians.

The Cherokees needed guns and lead and powder to repel the Chickasaws. They were offered ten thousand English pounds sterling in the trading goods they hoped would help them. In return they were to give up more land. The goods would be guns and ammunition, for the most part. Or, instead, they could have taken two thousand pounds sterling in cash. But money was of little use to them. It was manufactured goods they wanted and no one could supply them except the English.

There was conflict in the councils. Nancy Ward—Ghigau, the "Beloved Woman"—agreed with the old chiefs, Oconostota and Attakullaculla. They believed that the Cherokees must have the means to defend themselves against the Chickasaws.

Nancy was Attakullaculla's niece. His son, Dragging Canoe, wanted the weapons too, but he opposed the transfer of more land to get them. He wanted to make war on the white settlers in the area of the Watauga River. This meant taking the side of the English in their struggle with the colonials. These differing views split the family as they did many other families.

The trade was made. The Cumberland Valley—all of the

vast lands between the Kentucky River on the north and the
south watershed of the Cumberland, and a path to these lands
from the east—went to the Transylvania Company. It was all
of Kentucky and most of central Tennessee. It was land also
claimed by the Shawnees and the Iroquois.

Chief Dragging Canoe wanted the guns and ammunition,
but he violently disagreed with the trade. Boiling with rage, he
declared, "Kentucky will be a dark and bloody ground!"

Nancy Ward said, "Perhaps peace will come. With proper
weapons we can defend ourselves from the Chickasaws. But we
need not fight the white settlers. Perhaps we can persuade
those who have built their cabins on the Watauga to leave our
land."

"It will not do! We must fight those *unakas*, those whites, on
the Watauga. They will never leave!"

"The white settlers are no worse for us than the English.
They may be better. We have always fought for England. It has
done us no good. They have taken our land. Now a fresh wind
is blowing toward us. The American colonists are beginning to
resist the English. They want something better. They may win.
If they do, perhaps the Cherokees can win too. Win with them.
I want peace. But if we can have no peace, we should fight for
something better."

"The *unakas* are already on the Watauga River!" Dragging
Canoe shouted.

"True. But it is a small river. Perhaps we can arrange that

they come no farther. But the English! We have given them all the land between two great rivers so we can buy weapons to protect ourselves from our enemies, the Chickasaws," Nancy replied.

Then Cornstalk, a Shawnee chief, came with Mohawks, Delawares, and Ottawas to the Cherokee towns. They were from the north and they were allies of the English. They urged war against the Americans, against the white settlers along the Watauga River.

Nancy Ward's voice was heard in the councils. She protested against war with the Americans. And she wanted no war with the English. She spoke for peace.

Chapter 7

WAR

A GREAT council was called in Chota. Chiefs and braves and women came from all of the Cherokee towns. It was May, 1776.

At a nod from Chief Attakullaculla, the Shawnee chief, Cornstalk, rose and faced the Cherokees. "My brothers," he said, "the white people are at war with themselves. Those on the frontier who invade your land are at war with their King from across the sea."

"You say they fight among themselves?" asked Chief Oconostota.

"It is true. And now is our great opportunity."

"How can their war be our opportunity?" asked Attakullaculla.

"The English from across the sea have always brought trade to us. The Americans have brought us nothing but raids and war at our borders. They have stolen our land."

"That is true," said Oconostota.

"But is it all of the truth?" asked Nancy Ward.

"It is true!" interrupted Dragging Canoe. "We should make war on them! There is no good in the white man for the red man. Strike the war pole!"

"We can trust the English King. Fall upon the Americans. The English have always supplied us with trade goods. The Americans have no factories. They cannot sell us guns and blankets."

"Can we expect fairness from the English King?" asked Nancy. "Within the past year the English found us in distress and took the valley of the Cumberland River from us. Each year they have demanded more and yet more of our land because our people want their trade goods—and their whisky," she added sadly. "We have surrendered our land to them. We have always been asked for our land, our strength, and our blood. In return we have received only manufactured goods, alcohol, and disease."

"It is true. What Ghigau says is true," said Chief Attakulla-culla. "Once we did not need their manufactured goods. Once our people lived by their own hands, their own skills. But now they want all these foreign goods."

"But what can we do?" asked Chief Oconostota. "The outside world is sweeping in on us from all directions."

"We have tried war. We have tried to satisfy them. We have

given them land. We have fought their battles. Now we must try peace," said Nancy.

"No!" shouted Bloody Fellow. "Dragging Canoe is right! Kill the American settlers on the Watauga!"

"And on the Holston and the Nolichucky!" Raven cried.

"Hear me," Nancy said. "All of the white people we once knew as Englishmen. Now they are at war. The settlers must be thought of as Americans. There are those among them who think as the English King thinks. They are called Tories. They want to remain English. Let us not divide ourselves. Let us all remain Cherokees, intent on our own liberty. Let us remain at peace. But if that is impossible, if we must fight, let it be with the Americans. They fight for change, for something different, for something better. Let us do the same."

Henry Stuart, an agent of the English King, spoke up. He turned toward Dragging Canoe and said, "One hundred horses loaded with ammunition will come to you from the King's warehouses in Florida. We will support you. But your care must be great to distinguish the King's enemies from the King's friends. We must try to save the Royalists—the Tories—on the frontier."

"Now is the time to begin! There is no time to be lost," Cornstalk urged.

"We are not helpless!" cried Dragging Canoe. "We can do what has been done to us. The Americans are our enemies! We must fight!"

The war party was loud. Their shouts for war filled the air.

Doublehead, Bloody Fellow, Osiotto, Young Tassel, Abraham, Raven, and other hotheaded young chiefs and warriors took up the cry.

"War!"

"Take hair and horses!"

"War! Scalps and horses!"

"Take up the hatchet!"

"Raid! Take guns and booty!"

"War!"

"Death to the *unakas*! To the white people!"

"Strike the war pole!"

"War!"

Chapter 8

THE "BLACK DRINK"

IT WAS a sad time for Nancy Ward. She knew that war could do no good for the Cherokees.

She was alone now, a widow for the second time. With her children she was making her way, operating a rapidly growing and successful farm. She was not alone in her notions that war solved no problems. Chiefs Attakullaculla and Oconostota, both old now, joined with her. A few others were with her too. But their voices were almost smothered in the hot-bloods' eagerness for battle. There was deep division among the Cherokees. Both men and women were divided in their views.

Jarrett Williams, Isaac Thomas, and William Fawling were traders, working in Chota. Their homes were in the American settlements. They sympathized with the American cause and opposed the English King. Dragging Canoe and his friends, eager for war against the Americans, seized the three traders and their merchandise, the first prizes of the war.

The three traders were put in the stockade while the war party prepared for real action. They planned to raid the cabins of the American settlers on the Holston River near Long Island and the small settlements at the Virginia border. They would descend on the settlers on the Nolichucky River, in Carter's Valley, and at Fort Watauga.

It was July 8, 1776. The raids would be on July 20. The Cherokees did not yet know that the American Declaration of Independence had been signed on July 4.

A sad duty came to Ghigau. Although she felt it was a mistake to make the raids, she held a high office and tradition required that she prepare the "black drink" for the braves to take to purify themselves for battle. Perhaps it would help prevent injury and loss of life.

Radiant in white deerskin clothes, trimmed in white swans'-down, she appeared before the war fire. The war kettle was on the blaze. She had filled it with water brought from the river.

Each of her motions was from the traditions of her people and each of her actions was marked with a sweep of a white swan's wing, now slow and graceful, now fast and sharp.

Chanting ancient songs, she moved around the fire, the swan's wing always restless, always moving.

She drew a handful of salt from a deerskin bag that fell from her shoulder, and threw it at the feet of Dragging Canoe, the war chief. She turned and scattered salt on the fire.

Feeling ran high in the crowd. Another solemn moment in the ritual was at hand.

Slowly, Nancy took leaves of the yaupon from her bag. They had come from a holly shrub that grew on the sacred hills of the Cherokees. She threw the leaves into the kettle. There they would simmer and the "black drink" would be made ready for the warriors.

Chapter 9

THE ESCAPE

NANCY WARD was part English, but she was a Cherokee. She wanted to assist her people. How could she? What could she do that might help them? What could she do to bring peace?

Night deepened. The warriors were ready for battle. They had taken the "black drink." War dances were being performed. War songs, war cries rang out defiantly into the darkness.

When her ceremonial duties had been performed, Nancy, and many others of the peace party, had gone to their homes. They had done all they could for the impatient warriors.

The war songs troubled her. She stepped out of her house and looked into the black of night. There was no movement except the leaves in the trees. The whippoorwills were sounding their sharp, clear song. She knew what she must do.

Quickly she went inside and collected a packet of provisions. Then, in the dark, she moved away, toward the stockade where the three traders were held prisoners. She slipped cautiously through the shadows, stopped and listened. Her eyes, now accustomed to the darkness, could see no one. There were no guards. Good. They were at the war dance.

She caught her breath. The war dance could well turn into a dance of death for the three traders. She must act quickly.

At the stockade she stopped and listened. She heard soft voices inside. She made a low sound, "Hssst. Hssst."

"What's that? Who's there?"

"It is Nancy Ward."

"What is it, Nancy?"

"I have a rope. I will throw it over the stockade wall. You must leave. At once."

She loosened the coil in her hand. Holding one end, she threw it over the tall, close-set posts. Making a half-hitch on the post near the gate, she held it tight.

In a few moments three men were at her side. "Come. Follow me," she whispered. Four dark shadows moved away and soon were in the woods at the end of the town.

They huddled close together in the darkness. "Dragging Canoe plans war," she said softly.

"Sounds like he's going to have it," Isaac Thomas said.

"Many of our people follow him."

"We been hearin' the war dances," said Jarrett Williams.

"We were wonderin' if they might make for us first," said Isaac.

"It is possible," Nancy answered. "But you are safe now, I hope. Dragging Canoe, Abraham, and Raven will lead three raiding parties."

"Three? Sounds like it's going to be a real war," said William.

"It is. There will be over seven hundred men."

"Great Scott!"

"Yes. They will attack the fort on the Watauga, the settlements near Long Island on the Holston, and those on the Nolichucky and in Carter's Valley. You must go and warn them."

"Why do you tell us this, Nancy?" asked Isaac.

"Do you expect a trap?" Nancy replied. "Do you feel that I am helping you to escape so they can kill you?"

"Well—" Isaac did not finish his answer.

"They could kill you right here. Indeed they may try. We have all known each other for years, but I can't blame you for wondering," Nancy said.

"I'm sorry," Isaac said.

"It's all right. But it is no trap. It is only that I am opposed to war. If I must take a side, it will be with the Americans. I want for my people the same things the Americans want for themselves—freedom to live our own lives."

"Amen to that," said Isaac.

"I hope you can reach the settlements in time to warn them." There was a pause, then Nancy continued. "I am not against my people. I am sure you love the Cherokees, as I do. We have worked together for so long. I hope that the warning I give you will save the lives of Cherokees as well as the *unakas*, the white settlers."

"I know how you feel. I am part Cherokee too. These are my people," said William Fawling.

Nancy tried to explain again. "The voice of peace is hard to hear above the cry of war," she said.

"So it is," Jarrett Williams agreed.

"I have searched my heart," said Nancy. "This is all that is left for me to do for my people. With war hot in the blood, they might seek to kill you tonight. You are good traders. You have sold my people the things they need and want. You have been fair to us. Perhaps you can help guide the Americans to fairness too. But there is no more time for talk. Go now. Tell the settlers the raids will come on July 20. You will have time. Be careful."

"Bless you, Nancy," said Jarrett.

"Bless you," William repeated.

"Tell the American settlers that many of us—many Cherokees—want peace. Here is food for you. You will need it on your journey."

Nancy thrust a small package into the hands of each man. "Now go. And good luck," she said.

Chapter 10

MRS. BEAN

THE RAIDS were over. The warriors returned to Chota.

Dragging Canoe had been wounded. Early in the first attack, a settler's rifle ball had gone through both legs at the thighs.

"Most settlers were in the forts. They had left their cabins," explained Raven. "Some had gone away. We could not find them."

"We got some. There are scalps," cried Bloody Fellow.

"We took losses," said Young Tassel.

Old men, women, and children came close to the returning warriors. Whose son had not come back? Whose husband? Whose father? As the news spread of the dead and missing, cries of sorrow rose, wails of grief.

"We burned cabins," Bloody Fellow said proudly.

"But they had taken almost everything as they escaped," a warrior complained.

"There was little or nothing left," another growled.

Nancy Ward turned away. She had heard enough. It was clear that she had saved many lives on both sides. The horrible massacre that had been planned had failed.

She had seen the wounded warriors and Dragging Canoe on his litter. She had caught a glimpse of the few forlorn American prisoners the Indians had captured during the raids. She felt sorry because of the damage that had been done, but she felt no need to see or hear more. She turned toward her house.

"But there are prisoners," Abraham boasted.

Among the captives was a woman, Mrs. Bean. The usual fate of such prisoners was to become slaves.

Abraham continued, "I captured the woman as she was going to the fort. She was driving cows. All the other people had gone ahead of her, but she stayed behind to drive her cows." He shoved his rifle against Mrs. Bean.

"The woman was slow, like her cows," cried Doublehead.

"Yes. She's a milk drinker," said Young Tassel.

"It took quick action," said Abraham, not wanting honor to escape him. There was little honor in taking a woman prisoner, but Abraham thought he might make it so by boasting and talking in a loud voice.

Other warriors were boasting too of their feats, but no great pride came to the Cherokees. Rage grew instead, and rage might take the place of honor as well as grief.

The crowd seized Mrs. Bean. Perhaps the woman could give

them what they were seeking—revenge and comfort for their feelings of failure.

Nancy Ward, in her kitchen, had turned to work to relieve her troubled mind. The boasting voices of the warriors, the angry shouts of the people seemed louder, more urgent, growing more violent.

She opened the wooden chest near the fireplace and seized her white swan's wing. She threw a narrow shawl of swans'-down over her shoulders and rushed out of the house and down the road.

Nancy pushed her way through the excited mob. At its center was the woman, Mrs. Bean, tied to a stake. Faggots had been piled on the ground at her feet. A blazing torch was in a warrior's hand.

"Stop!" Nancy cried. She was the Ghigau now, the "Beloved Woman." The sacred swans'-down on her shoulders fluttered as the breeze touched it, a snow-white carpet for the beautiful, regal head rising above it.

The Ghigau's swan's wing, powerful medicine, was in her hand. She moved it through the air with a wide, sweeping gesture.

"Cherokees! Listen to me!" she demanded. "Have you not had enough? Sorrow will not be cured with rage! Killing cannot produce honor or glory! Violence cannot take the place of failure! Let your tears flow for those who have not returned, but hold your hand still. Your reason has gone. Let it come

back. You do violence to the Great Spirit who guards us all!"

The swan's wing paused in its flight and pointed at the warrior who held the flaming torch. It stopped his arm. He dropped the living fire to the bare ground at his feet.

The swan's wing moved again. Now it pointed at Mrs. Bean. It stabbed the air. "Cut the cords that bind her! Free her—now!"

A knife flashed. The cords loosened and fell.

Nancy stepped forward and helped the woman through the pile of wood. The hand that held the swan's wing was around Mrs. Bean now.

The mob parted before the two women. Slowly Nancy and the trembling, tear-stained woman made their way up the dirt street, leaving a silent crowd behind them.

Chapter 11

COWS FOR THE CHEROKEES

In a few days Mrs. Bean was over the shock of her ordeal, though she could never dismiss it from her mind.

A frontier woman and the wife of William Bean, she was accustomed to be wary of Indians. Mr. Bean was a captain in the militia. He was a friend of Daniel Boone and had been the first settler in the Watauga district. Their son Russell was the first white child born in the area that later became the state of Tennessee.

Mrs. Bean was surprised to find that Nancy Ward was a delightful woman, a charming companion, and an excellent housekeeper. She operated her farm efficiently and her house was well furnished. There was an air of prosperity about it that was not found in the frontier settlements of the whites.

Nancy stood erect. She was a beautiful woman, with a prominent nose, regular features, and clear complexion. Her hair

was black and soft, her eyes large, piercing, black, and her
motions regal. She commanded respect and love from family,
friends, and servants of her household.

The two women grew close during the weeks Nancy was
looking for a way to return Mrs. Bean to her home through the
wild, war-torn country that separated Chota from the American settlements.

"How will I ever get home?" asked Mrs. Bean.

"Dragging Canoe and his people have gone south to the
Chickamauga Creek. Other Cherokees who want to take sides
with the English are going there. They are becoming known as
the Chickamauga Cherokees."

"Will the war ever stop?"

"Sometime, yes. So much evil comes from war. It extends
everywhere, past injury, death, and destruction of property. It
wrecks family life too. Dragging Canoe is my cousin. He op-
poses his father, Chief Attakullaculla. Each of us has allies,
people who share our views. Each has his followers."

"It is true with us too. We have Royalists, or Tories, who
favor the King. Already I have lost some of my old friends."

"In the meantime, I suppose we must go on. We must do the
best we can, as we see it," said Nancy. She was silent for a
moment. "There are but few things worth making war for. One
of them is freedom, liberty, the right to live your own life in
your own home, in your own way. That, I take it, is what your
American Revolution is for. I hope so. If such views prevail,

the Cherokees should enjoy them too. We are the first Americans." She smiled.

"So you are." Mrs. Bean met Nancy's eyes. She smiled back at her.

"Don't you worry. I will find a way to get you back to your home and family before the war is over," Nancy said.

"I will be so glad to see them. And my cows too. Oh, I hope nothing has happened to my cows," Mrs. Bean said fervently.

"Why did you pause to drive them? You would have to go so slowly."

"I had to try to save my cows," said Mrs. Bean.

"You could have run to the fort and saved yourself, couldn't you?"

"I suppose so. But I couldn't leave them."

"Why?" Nancy inquired.

"Their milk. It is so good for children."

"But there is mother's milk," said Nancy.

"Of course, for babies. But often there is not enough. And then, there are the older children. The adults too. Cows and their milk are very valuable."

"I don't know about it," said Nancy. "The traders don't offer cows for sale. Nor milk. In the raids, I am told the warriors kill the cows first thing."

"Why, in heaven's name?"

"They make noise. They—they—"

"They low?" asked Mrs. Bean helpfully.

"If that's what you call it. The noise warns people."

"What a shame!" Mrs. Bean exclaimed.

"Then too," said Nancy, "the cows are slow-moving animals. The warriors believe that one who eats their meat will grow to move slowly too."

"It's a shame. A downright shame!" Mrs. Bean cried. She caught herself. She didn't want to insult her hostess, the woman who had saved her. She didn't want to be rude and make light of Cherokee beliefs.

"I don't mean to criticize the customs or the legends of the Cherokees. But I am sure they are mistaken."

"It could be. Men are very foolish sometimes," Nancy added, smiling.

"Cattle have been considered to be of great value since the beginning of civilization," Mrs. Bean continued quietly.

"Cows too?" asked Nancy.

"Especially cows. From cows there is meat, of course, as well as milk. And from milk comes cream and butter and cheese. These are nourishing, valuable foods—and they are delicious to the taste."

"Tell me about butter and cheese," Nancy said seriously. "Tell me about cows." She sat down.

Mrs. Bean sat beside her. She told Nancy of the value of dairy products and of the methods of making and using butter and cheese.

When she had finished Nancy stood up. She was serious and

determined, as when she commanded the release of Mrs. Bean from the stake. "We must have cows," she said.

The cattle were quick to come. Hunters drove in those which had escaped from the settlers. Nancy purchased some of the best cows that could be found. The Cherokees raised corn and there was fodder for the cows. Grass was abundant.

With Mrs. Bean as a teacher, the Cherokee women and their servants learned to milk the cows. The magic of cheese and butter-making became known.

It came time for Mrs. Bean to leave the Cherokee town and return to her family. Little Fellow and Nancy's son, Five Killer, were going to escort her.

Mrs. Bean tried to express her thanks. "I only did what was right," said Nancy. "But you have helped our whole nation. You have taught us the great benefits of cows."

"My dear, it is you who have done it," said Mrs. Bean. "You have brought knowledge to your people which will benefit them forever."

Chapter 12

A GIFT

On December 16, 1780, the American militiamen met the Chickamauga Cherokees in the Battle of Boyd's Creek. Dragging Canoe, and the others who felt as he did, fought the Americans relentlessly.

The Americans won the battle and they waited for two other groups of soldiers to join them in a final push against the Chickamauga Cherokees. It was cold and the Americans were out of food. There was no game. The men lived on what wild nuts, frozen haws, and grapes they could find and small rations of parched corn. The place was known as "Hungry Camp."

Finally, when they were all gathered together, there was an army of over seven hundred men. Hunger continued.

On Christmas Day, Nancy Ward rode to the quarters of the American colonel, Arthur Campbell. The colonel invited her to dismount. "What can I do for you, Nancy?" he asked.

"I have come to ask you to make peace," she replied.

"We are at war with the Cherokees," he said.

"With the Chickamauga Cherokees," she corrected him.

"When you see an Indian in these parts, it is kind of difficult to tell whether he is a Chickamauga Cherokee or not," Colonel Campbell said pleasantly.

"I know. It is the same as trying to tell a Royalist or a Tory from an American patriot," she answered.

"Exactly. I know there are many Cherokees who do not approve of what Dragging Canoe is doing. I know that you are one of them. I know that you have often helped us, and so have other Cherokees. We will not attack you. We will protect you."

"I am not concerned about myself. All of my people are in my thoughts," Nancy declared.

"Dragging Canoe too?"

"I want peace for him too, for all the Chickamauga Cherokees, for all of us. But he did not send me here to talk to you. A number of other chiefs did. We have a peace party as well as a war party." She spoke earnestly.

"It is Dragging Canoe and his warriors who are our enemies," the colonel answered. "I must destroy the Chickamauga Cherokees who make war on us. Those who live in Hiwassee and Chestowee, and those along Chickamauga Creek."

"Perhaps they will stop fighting if you do."

"Perhaps? Can you guarantee that they will keep the peace? That they will stop making war on us?"

"No, I can't guarantee that. But they are tired. Their women and children are overcome with the pain of war." Nancy's voice was clear. Her eyes sought the colonel's for a sign of understanding.

He returned her gaze. "I can't do it, Nancy. I can't take the chance. It will be all I can do to try to get my men to distinguish good Indians from bad ones. I must try to overcome the Chickamauga Cherokees and knock them out of the war. They are ravaging our western frontier."

"Stay here. Don't go against them. Perhaps they will drop the hatchet," she pleaded.

"They have had plenty of chances for that. I cannot delay. My men are hungry. I am far away from supplies. I must fight it out as soon as possible and turn my men to the east where the Continental army needs help."

"Your men are hungry?" she asked.

"Starving."

It was a strange confession for a military leader to make to a Cherokee woman. A word from her would fortify the Chickamauga ambitions, and allow them to fight the militiamen with the knowledge that they were fighting a starving opponent. Colonel Campbell displayed enormous confidence in Nancy Ward.

His confidence was not misplaced. That day, after Nancy returned to Chota, she ordered a herd of her cattle to be driven to the starving troops. The American soldiers fed well on the meat.

On December 28, the unmistakable hatred of the American frontier militiamen for all Indians was made clear. They set fire to the Cherokee villages of Chota and Tellico, as well as the towns of the Chickamaugas and Chestowee and Hiwassee.

In the battles, Nancy Ward and her family were taken into custody. They were well protected.

On February 17, 1781, Thomas Jefferson, then the governor of Virginia, wrote to the militia commander: "Nancy Ward seems rather to have taken refuge with you. In this case, her inclination ought to be followed as to what is done with her."

The governor was well aware that all Cherokees were not opposed to the Americans. The Cherokees rebuilt their towns and Nancy Ward returned to take up her life in Chota.

Chapter 13

A REPORT TO
GOVERNOR JEFFERSON

THERE WAS still a war party and a peace party among the Cherokees.

There were those in the American forces who sought peace with the Cherokees. They deplored Colonel Arthur Campbell's vigorous raids against the Chickamaugas and his destruction of the Cherokee towns.

Colonel William Fleming of the Virginia Militia had fought with the English in the French and Indian Wars. He was experienced in Indian affairs. On January 19, 1781, he wrote a report to Governor Thomas Jefferson. In his report, Colonel Fleming agreed with the views of Joseph Martin, also of the Virginia Militia, that the military raids against the Cherokees were unwise: "The burning of their huts, and destruction of their corn, will I fear make the whole Nation Our irreconcilable Enemies, and force them for Sustenance to live altogether by depredation on our frontiers. . . ."

Colonel Fleming sent Jefferson a statement by William Springstone, formerly a trader and an interpreter to the Virginia agent for Indian affairs.

Mr. Springstone said that in November, 1880, Chief Raven had made a treaty with the British agent. Raven agreed to make war on Virginia and Carolina and to fight American traders. England would pay Raven for prisoners and their horses. He reported that settlers had already been killed and taken prisoner and their horses stolen. Raven also told Springstone that he and John Martin and others were to be put to death.

Some of Raven's plans met with failure because there were people within the ranks of the Cherokees who favored peace and were eager to assist the Americans.

And Springstone happily wrote that he and four American traders had escaped from death at the hands of Raven's warriors "with the advice of some Indian friends and the Assistance of Nancy Ward with other Indian women. . . ."

Chapter 14

A MOTHER SPEAKS

A MESSAGE came from the Americans. A Commission had been appointed to treat with the Indians for peace. The meeting was to be held at Long Island on the Holston River on July 20, 1781.

Long speeches were made. When Captain John Sevier spoke he said, "We are here to talk of treaties."

"We have received bad advice from the British," said Young Tassel, one of the Cherokee chiefs.

"I have never hated the Cherokees. I had to fight them for the safety of my people," Sevier replied.

The speeches went on and on. Then a strange thing happened. It had never occurred before. While Indian women had power and authority in their own councils, no woman had ever before spoken at a treaty council with white men.

Nancy Ward rose. She was in ceremonial dress, white deer-

skin trimmed with swans'-down, and she held her swan's wing, symbol of her authority.

She spoke quietly, earnestly. Her voice showed the deep emotion she felt. She said, "You know that women are always looked upon as nothing; but we are your mothers, you are our sons. Our cry is all for peace; let it continue. This peace must last forever. Let your women's sons be ours, our sons be yours. Let your women hear our words."

The Commissioners, all soldiers, knew of Nancy Ward's actions. They knew of the rescue of Mrs. Bean and of the traders and other Americans during the war. They knew of her warning of the Holston and the Watauga raids, and of still other attacks against the white settlers. They knew of her introduction of cows and milk to the Cherokees. They knew too of her gift of her cattle to help the starving militiamen.

As the Commissioners listened, they pushed back their lust for Indian lands. They well knew of the great debts they owed to Nancy Ward.

They were humbled by her words. The idea she expressed touched their hearts for the moment and pushed their greed aside. They selected Colonel William Christian to reply. The colonel had fought against the Chickamauga Cherokees, but he was a rare officer who had often protected Cherokee Indians and the women and children of other tribes.

Colonel Christian stood solemnly before the treaty council. He too spoke quietly, thoughtfully: "We have listened well to your talk; it is humane . . . No man can hear it without being moved by it. Such words and thought show the world that human nature is the same everywhere. Our women shall hear your words, and we know how they will feel and think of them. . . . We will not meddle with your people if they will be still and quiet at home and let us live in peace."

Nancy's words had been effective. The Americans made a treaty of peace, and they did not make any demands for Indian lands. Not then. They were glad to be free of Indian raids. A pause in this war would give them opportunity to fight the British elsewhere.

The treaty gave the militia a chance to move a detachment of troops to fight with General George Washington's army against General Cornwallis in the last campaign of the American Revolution. They fought in the last battle at Yorktown, Virginia, and were present at the British surrender on October 19, 1781.

History would show that the plea of Nancy Ward would not be long lasting. The fine words of Colonel Christian would soon be forgotten or ignored.

There would be more treaties and more promises. The Americans and the Cherokees would fight, until at last, the Cherokees would suffer defeat and would be sent away from their beloved lands.

Chapter 15

FAIR TRADING

IN THE FOLLOWING years Nancy continued in her efforts to promote peace between the Cherokees and the American states. Chota remained a "City of Refuge." Her home was open to those in need. She prospered. Her farm was fat with the products of peace and diligent work.

In 1783, William Rankin and Jeremiah Jack, two traders from the Nolichucky River area went on a trading expedition to the Cherokees. The winter had been hard. Corn in the white settlements was gone. Starvation faced the settlers. The traders wanted to exchange clothing for corn.

They encountered a group of Indians who did not respond to notions of trade. Scars of the war remained. Instead, they were disorderly and restless. They seemed intent on injury to the traders and theft of the clothing.

Jack and Rankin raised their guns to resist. The Indians'

weapons moved restlessly. Reason had gone. Words of anger flashed back and forth and were ready to explode.

Before a shot could be fired, Nancy Ward came between the angry men. She did not wear the swans'-down, nor did she have her swan's wing.

She seemed to grow taller as she spoke words of reason. "Trade. Do not make war," she said. "The white men are our brothers. The same house holds us. The same sky covers us all. The Cherokees have corn. The white men want it. They have clothing. You want that. Is it not better to exchange your goods fairly than to trade lead balls from smoking weapons and the blood they will find in both white and red bodies?"

The ready muzzles of the guns were lowered.

"Cherokees are as good at trading as the white men are. Do not drug yourselves with whisky and you will make good deals," Nancy said.

While Nancy Ward watched, the exchanges were made. The Indians and the traders were satisfied and they parted as friends.

Chapter 16

A PIPE OF PEACE

ON NOVEMBER 28, 1785, the time came for another effort to settle the disputes that continued between the whites and the Indians. Several treaties with the states of Georgia, South Carolina, and North Carolina had failed. It was time for the Federal government to act.

A treaty-making council was called at Hopewell on the Keowee River in South Carolina. The council lasted for ten days, and the treaty was signed by twenty-seven chiefs.

Once again Nancy Ward spoke to the treaty Commissioners. She spoke for those who were not warriors. She spoke for the women and the quiet people who sought peace instead of war.

"I am fond of hearing that there is peace. I hope that you have taken us by the hand in real friendship. I have a pipe and a little tobacco to give the Commissioners to smoke in friendship. I look upon you and the red people as my children. Your having determined on peace is most pleasing to me, for I have

seen much trouble during the late war. I am old, but I hope yet
to bear children, who will grow up and people our nation, as
we are now to be under the protection of Congress and shall
have no more disturbance.

"The talk I have given is from the young warriors I have
raised in my town, as well as myself. They rejoice that we have
peace, and we hope the chain of friendship will never more be
broken."

When she had finished, Nancy walked to the Commissioners
and handed them two strings of wampum as a symbol of peace.
Then she presented them with a pipe and tobacco to use in
fulfilling one of the honored traditions of her people.

Chapter 17

THE WOMEN SPEAK

NANCY'S DAUGHTER, Elizabeth, married Joseph Martin, who was an agent for North Carolina to the Cherokees. He had been active in the militia and was promoted through the ranks to general in the Virginia Militia. Betsy had a fine estate at Wakhovee on the south side of Hiwassee River fifty miles from Tellico Blockhouse.

William, General Martin's white son of a prior marriage, described Nancy Ward as "one of the most superior women I ever saw."

Nancy's other daughter, Catharine, married John Walker. Five Killer and Little Fellow, her sons, found Cherokee wives. They became chiefs and lived in small towns near Chota. Five Killer, like his mother, was a leading advocate for peace, although in 1813 he fought with Colonel Gideon Morgan's raiders against the Creeks. This was part of the War of 1812 when the Cherokees allied themselves with the United States under General Andrew Jackson against the British.

The Cherokees felt that their help in this war against England would assure them of the friendship of the United States and would guarantee them the peaceful occupancy of the land then remaining to them. Their hopes failed when General Jackson did not support their claims to the land they had occupied ever since it was given to them by the Great Spirit.

The Cherokees now became engaged in the last chapter of their losing contest. It would be long and distressing, and it would last until 1839. The policy of the United States government called for the removal of the Cherokees west, first to Arkansas and later, to Oklahoma. Some of the Indians went, in an effort to escape from the pressures of the government and of Georgia. Others refused to go and declared that they would part with no more land.

During these tumultuous years of conflict and change, Nancy Ward continued to occupy the place she had made for herself as an honored and respected leader of the Cherokees.

In May, 1817, the Cherokees met in council to consider the adoption of a constitution like that of the United States, and to debate the idea of moving west.

Illness and age made it impossible for Nancy to attend. But she still had a voice in the council and she would use it. Neither distance, nor health, nor her years could stop her.

Nancy sent her walking stick to the council as a symbol of

her interest and presence. A letter went with it. It bore not only her signature, but also those of twelve other Cherokee women.

The letter gave this advice: "The Cherokee ladys . . . have thought it their duty as mothers to address their beloved chiefs and warriors. . . . We have raised all of you on the land which we now have, which God gave us to inhabit. . . . We do not wish to go to an unknown country. . . . Your mothers, your sisters ask and beg of you not to part with any more of our lands. . . . Keep it for our growing children, for it was the good will of our Creator to place us here. . . ."

And the warning was given not to make any more treaties with the whites: "Keep your hands off of paper talks."

Nancy emphasized the need to keep their land: "Therefore, children, don't part with any more of our lands but continue on it and enlarge your farms and cultivate and raise corn and cotton and we, your mothers and sisters, will make clothing for you. . . . It was our desire to forewarn you all not to part with our lands."

She closed her letter with these words: "Nancy Ward to her children warriors to take pity and listen to the talks of your sisters. . . . I have a great many grandchildren which I wish them to do well on our land."

Chapter 18

NANCY WARD'S LEGACY

IN THE Revolutionary War, Nancy Ward took a place with the Americans in their desperate contest for independence and freedom. She and others sought peace, but with arms, fire, anger, revenge, fear, ambition, and death at every hand, she took a side. The success of the Americans might bring independence and freedom for the Cherokees too.

She helped American soldiers, traders, and settlers whenever and wherever she could. It was welcome assistance, gratefully received at the time.

But Nancy's hopes were not fulfilled. Her wartime efforts were forgotten. The American goals were achieved, but Nancy's were ignored. Time and history failed her.

After the war, the new American nation and its states continued to close in upon the Cherokees. More treaties and promises were made and broken. The Cherokees continued to lose their land.

In 1819, the relentless pressures of the United States brought yet another treaty. It was called the Hiwassee Purchase. The land in the valley of the Little Tennessee River was taken.

Nancy's home and the town of Chota were now gone. The Cherokees had to move, even those who had helped the Americans. Mostly they moved south, toward Chickamauga, and created new towns.

Nancy moved to the Ocoee River at a place called Woman Killer Ford. There she operated an inn. Now known as Granny Ford, she made her inn a place of refuge where the weary and distressed were welcome. The spirit of Chota moved with her.

More farms and plantations were being developed. The Cherokee society was changing to one based on agriculture and business. Hunting grounds were disappearing. Some Indians continued in the old ways, but game was not plentiful as it once was. Farms kept the people well fed. Nancy Ward's introduction of the cow to her people was the foundation of a lasting change in Cherokee society.

Cherokee culture was changing in the image of the American ways. The Cherokees developed a government more suitable to the time. Slowly a new order began to form. Education among them was increased. Young men were being educated at Cornwall, Connecticut, and elsewhere. They brought a new force to their nation.

With the passing years, many Cherokees became discouraged and, seeking freedom to follow their own way of life, moved west to the borders of the Mississippi River. Most remained, to continue the struggle through the years, until finally, in a tremendous upheaval that lasted until 1839, the Cherokee Nation was forced to go beyond the Mississippi in a bitter march, marked by starvation and death. History calls it "The Trail of Tears." A few remained in their mountains, fugitives, for many years.

Whether they remained or moved west, the Cherokees continued their struggle, adjusting themselves to new conditions, striving for, and reaching, new goals. The courage and high spirit represented by Nancy Ward remained with them.

In 1821, a Cherokee named Sequoyah created a way of writing the Cherokee language. He had never been to school, yet by diligent thought and hard work, using a system he developed himself, he devised a system of putting Cherokee words down on paper. Within a few years the ability to read and write was common among his people. By 1825, there was a Cherokee newspaper.

The year 1822 was the year that marked the end for Nancy Ward. The last Ghigau, the last "Beloved Woman" of the Cherokees died. She was buried near Benton, Tennessee.

Those who were in the room saw a pale light rise from her body as her last breath came. The light was white, like swans'-down. It grew stronger and began to turn in small circles, fluttering as a young bird flutters its wings.

At last, as though reluctant to leave, it passed through the open door. It hesitated for a time, passing back and forth in front of the house. Then it rose high in the air. It became larger. Its form grew more distinct. Now it seemed to be a white swan. Spreading wings wide, it flew over the trees and the hill, past the distant ridges, toward Chota, the "City of Refuge."

INDEX

THE AUTHOR

Harold W. Felton, a lawyer by profession, is an author known for his tall tales and his biographies for young readers. A long-time interest in American folklore and history led to his first book, an anthology of legends about Paul Bunyan, and he has since written about all the major folklore characters, from Pecos Bill, John Henry, and Mike Fink to Fire-Fightin' Mose and Gib Morgan. His biographies include Jim Beckwourth, Edward Rose, Elizabeth Freeman, Nat Love, James Weldon Johnson, and Ely S. Parker.

Mr. Felton was born in the Midwest, but has long been a resident of New York City. He and his wife now have a home in Falls Village, Connecticut, where he devotes his leisure time to writing for young people.

THE ILLUSTRATOR

Carolyn Bertrand was born in Houston, Texas, and began her art studies there, winning scholarships at the art museum while still in high school. Later she studied at the Pennsylvania Academy of Fine Arts and the Barnes Foundation in Merion, Pennsylvania.

While living in California, she became interested in the American Indian. Traveling to Arizona, New Mexico, and Old Mexico, she drew Indians in those areas, and readily found a market for her pictures and prints.

Carolyn Bertrand now lives and works in New York City. This is her first illustrated book.